Table Of Contents (TOC)

Introduction

Chapter 1: What is passive income?

Chapter 2: The benefits of passive income

Chapter 3: Advantages and disadvantages of passive income over active income

Chapter 4: Passive income from real estate properties

Chapter 5: Passive income from selling informational products

Chapter 6: Passive income from peer-to-peer lending

Chapter 7: Passive income from dividend stocks

Chapter 8: Passive income from websites and affiliate marketing

Chapter 9: Passive income from savings interests

Chapter 10: Where to start from?

__Conclusion__

Introduction

Many of us are experiencing issues with the amount of income that we generate. Or maybe, at some point, we simply get enough of our boss, we can't stand one more single day working on a daily basis from 9 to 5 or to receive orders from someone else.

Everybody wants to be free, to have a less stressful life, everybody wants to travel, to spend time with friends, family. In other words, to ENJOY LIFE.

Passive Income is the answer – it's the way you can achieve all of your goals and your freedom.

This book will show you exactly what to do and in what ways.

Chapter 1: What is Passive Income?

Do you really want to work 8 or even more hours from Mondays to Saturdays and get enough money only to survive in this chaotic world? You probably don't want that. Neither do I.

Working actively is a lot more tiring, a lot more stressful and a lot less profitable than having a passive business behind you. It literally does all the work for you – you invest / work once and you get paid for that work all the time – while you travel, while you sleep, while you have fun, while you are doing anything else. The more passive businesses that you have, the more money you make, the more you can invest and you will also achieve freedom.

Freedom is something very tricky in our days – the system "pretends" we are all free and we live in a free world, but it doesn't work that way.

We are all "imprisoned" somehow, not just physically (in a jail for criminals or thieves) – money is the other one thing that imprisons as – at home (because you don't afford too many things), at work (you have to work to earn your money) and the worst part is that we worry too much for money when it comes to working actively.

Passive income is the key to freedom, no more stress, no more hard working, it is the only way that you can enjoy life to the highest levels. Wouldn't it be wonderful to generate 5000$ while you travel to an exotic destination, relax yourself and do anything that you have wished for?

In other words, passive income is the income received on a regular basis that requires little effort to maintain it as soon as you have finished a project or a passive income stream. It mainly results from trade activities and rental activities.

Examples of passive income:

Selling software – why do you think Bill Gates is rich? He is mainly rich thanks to Microsoft which is a big company well known worldwide, but most of the profit of the company came from selling Windows. What's Windows? It's a digital licensed software which is sold every day worldwide and it brings him profit passively, right?

Royalties – there are places where you can sell products or digital products and you get a royalty – royalties are something like a commission. Amazon gives you royalties for example – you upload a digital book (Kindle book) and by selling it (passively) you will earn a royalty. The more books you have, the more money you will make.

Digital courses - you can gain a lot of knowledge on different niches and subjects and you can record yourself or the screen of you PC and create a digital course. You can sell it where you want on the web – http://shareaskill.com http://udemy.com or even on http://clickbank.com

Websites – you can earn money passively by creating a website and putting ads on it. You get traffic, you get people to click your ads – you make money. All of this without requiring any other maintenance.

Affiliate marketing – this also involves websites – you can advertise other people's products on different websites, bring traffic to your websites and you will get a commission. You can also create a digital product such as a digital course and give it to other affiliate marketers to advertise it for you – people will do the work for you – you will certainly earn a lot of money.

Real estate – this is the best long term passive income stream that you can own. Let's say you manage to generate a lot of money using the internet, but you want to have something physical too, something to rely on and which you can also resell if you want to invest in anything else.

Real estate investments won't bring you a big amount of money comparing to the money that you invest, but it definitely gives you a smaller amount of money as long as you own it – it gives you an amount of money no matter what.

 The internet can sometimes get tricky – it can involve competition, maybe somebody will try to hack your account and steal everything you have or who knows. You have to take everything into consideration. A wise person who wants to make a living out of Passive Income will have to be aware that he has to split his total passive income into multiple income streams.

YouTube and Social Media – these are the places where a lot of people make money – on Facebook and other social media platforms you share links, free stuff and people will go on YouTube and watch videos. YouTube is full of ads now and if you have dozens of interesting videos, people will watch them, will share them and you will get a

commission from the amount of money that has
been allocated to those ads. All of these passively.

Chapter 2: Benefits of passive income

Passive income has a large portofolio of benefits which apply directly to the owner.

1. Tax benefits: you can possibly take a loss on passive activities. When you have passive income, then no self-employment tax is owed. You do not need to rent a place to start a company, you do not have to pay nothing else than income tax. No additional charges or fees.

2. Recurring income – once you have made an investment, it will bring you passive income month after month, you have the possibility to reinvest it, to grow the total cash flow.

3. Low maintenance – there is no such thing as "100% passive income" – you will need to maintain the business that brings you passive income and sometimes to improve it or to upgrade it, but it's take a lot less time to do it if you compared it to an active income business.

4. Ticket to financial freedom – Nowadays we are imprisoned in our office, forced to save money so we can survive in this chaotic world, we are LIMITED because of money. When you will earn money passively, this means that your money, your investments will work for you. This means that you have a lot more time to enjoy, a lot less stressful tasks to do and so you will have a happier life without any hesitations. If you have a property which you want to rent, you will create a steady stream of predictable passive income. With the financial support that passive income provides, you can keep the property all the time and watch how its values grows – you also have the possibility to sell it at the best moment and reinvest your money, helping to maximize your profits.

5. Easy to start - Some of the means to acquire passive income such as an online business website are easy to start right away without the need to fight bureaucracy. Some passive incomes businesses can be started in the next hour and within a few weeks you will see positive results. I will discuss about the multiple ways of generating passive income in the next chapters.

6. Time Freedom – passive income allows you to enjoy time in another manner, you will have to forget about things like – "Oh, I will be late for

work" or "Ah, I have to finish something until tomorrow." – You can work whenever you want, wherever you want, how much you want. You will still need to make some effort for a great amount of passive income to come each month, but you can have a break at any time – you don't have a boss, you don't have a fixed schedule, you are absolutely FREE.

7. Possibility of fulfilling your dreams – passive income has the potential of making your dreams come true. A lot of people have hobbies, passions, curiosities which sometimes are left behind because there is no time or money for those. More money and more time mean that you can follow your dreams, see the places that you have ever wanted and enjoy what you have ever wanted.

8. Wide source of income – the most important and the most advisable thing about passive income and in fact, for every kind of income or business that you have, you will need to spread out (diversify) your income streams. Don't put all the eggs in one bag, the bag could fall accidentally and you will lose all of them. So, diversify your income – build websites, create courses, lend money online, buy real estate properties, create books, create

templates, do affiliate marketing and other lots of ways of passive income streams.

Chapter 3: Advantages and disadvantages of passive income over active income

Active income is the oldest way to make money since mankind. Each person has to work in order to survive, to pay his/her taxes and even to save money. As times have changed, the possibilities for generating money have changed. The modern era will be mainly focused on spreading, diversifying income into multiple streams.

Active income comes from job employment, commissions, job compensation and tips. Passive income has advantages and disadvantages (only a few).

The advantages of passive income over active income are:

1. Active control over the investment: the owner of the investments has the word in the day-to-day operations that would impact the success of his investment. Active income does not advocate for this since they are employed, thus depending on somebody else's company.

2. Favorable tax treatments: taxes in passive income can be deferred indefinitely. For example, real estate properties are traded for larger ones. Corporations can take tax deductions when they use their profits to invest in other passive investments. Active income has deductions that are less plentiful.

3. Longer generation period: the time in which you receive active income is limited. You will get old, you will lose your overall strength, you will not be able to work all of your life, you will have to retire at some point. Passive income mechanisms can continue to grow until you opt to quit or die. Your passive income streams can be left as legacy to your children or to someone else. For example, a real estate property can be rented for 100 years, with low maintenance – your children and grandchildren will benefit from it, if they don't sell it. Another example would be for books, courses or other programs which have rights. Those rights can be transferred and be available for a 70 year period. Comparing to active income, which stops at some point in your life, passive income can continue to generate money and even to grow bigger.

4. Little work: activities that earn passive income are cheap to maintain and require little effort while activities that bring active income require more efforts and maintenance.

5. Higher income in passive activities: passive activities make you earn more money since the investments are not fixed. Active income generation income methods generate fixed income, for example, when you are employed at a certain fixed salary.

Passive income allows for more investments and income generation than active income. You can expand faster and safer.

Disadvantages of passive income over active income:

1. Start-up capital: In some passive income businesses you need a starting capital for your future businesses, while in active income businesses you don't need the start-up capital. If you need a job as fast as possible, you will find it, you will get hired and you won't have to do anything else than work.

2. Risky investments: some of the passive income generation techniques are risky to engage in and

can result to downfall after a few months or years while active income generation techniques are less risky. Sometimes in life, if you don't take a shot, you won't benefit from anything. You will have to risk, but only by managing it wisely.

Chapter 4: Passive Income From Real Estate Properties

Some of the world's richest celebrities have made their fortunes by investing in real estate properties. You can invest in real estate properties to rent them or resell them to make nice money out of them.

You can rent a space that you own without any additional investments, or if you make some investments, they will be very low. From these rentals, you collect money each month without any maintenance.

Which properties you should buy

At first you have to focus where, when and what you should buy to obtain the maximum profit. You will also take into consideration other facts such as the population of the city in which you invest, how much money people have in that area, how the prices are for rent and for sale of the properties. There may be areas in which you invest a lot and you get a lower return than you would have got in other areas (this could be in the US, in the UK or in other country worldwide).

For example, in New York, an apartment costs somewhere from 200,000$ up to 10$ Million if it's a luxurious one. How much money can you earn if you invest 300,000$ into an apartment in New York knowing the average price for rentals for that type of property?

In average, the prices are somewhere from 1000$ to 3000$ for such a property. When you buy such an apartment take into consideration two important real estate rules:

- The 2% rule – this rules say that for an investment of 100,000$, you will have to generate 2% of that money each month, which would be 2000$/month. In some places, this rule would be difficult to achieve, so major investors take into consideration this rule, but sometimes even 1% is OK. If you have invested 300,000$ into an apartment, you will have to charge at least 3000$/month to achieve this goal.

Don't invest 300,000$ to charge 1000$/month rent, it will be really hard to take all the investment back fast.

- The 50% rule – this rule says that all of the taxes, maintenance and any other additional costs should not exceed 50% of all the money that you get from rent, the other 50% should be your profit. Remember – AT LEAST 50%.

So if you charge 3000$/month, in one year you will earn 3000$ x 12 months = 36000$. You shouldn't pay more than 18000$/year the taxes and maintenance of the property, but in case to earn more than 50%, the difference up to 50% save it for any interventions or maintenance issues that may occur over time.

If you invest 300,000$ in one apartment in New York and rent it with 3000$/month, you should get around 20,000$ net each year, so you will get all your money back in 15 years. It may sound a lot, but you have the property, you can rent it 15 years more, 30 years more, you can sell it for a bigger price. During a lifetime (let's say 30 years), you real estate property will bring you 600,000$ and if you want to sell it after 30 years, you will probably exceed 1,000,000$ out of 300,000$. Remember, this is a long term investment and it is the safest way to generate money passively.

You can choose other areas or countries to buy real estate properties. For example, in Romania, Europe, a 2 bedroom apartment costs in Bucharest (capital of Romania) around 60,000$ and you can rent it for 400-500$/month. So you can diversify the real estate properties by buying more rather than just one.

In the UK, in London, a 3 bedroom apartment in a house (a part of the house) which is 30 minutes away from the city center costs somewhere between 350,000 and 500,000 GBP (520,000$ to 741,000$). The rent for such a house is from 2500 to 5000 British Pounds which is 3700$ to 7400$.

These are just some examples. Make your own analysis and buy which you think it's best.

Real estate properties are recommended to invest in once you have other passive income businesses, once you have a lot of money and you don't want to risk it, waste it or put it into a bank account and get almost nothing, as the interest is getting lower and lower in our days.

Chapter 5: Passive Income From Selling Informational Products

Generating passive income out of books, CDs, DVDs or any kind of digital informational products is one of the easiest and fastest ways to start and grow your business.

For example, you can create eBooks and you can sell them on Amazon, Smashwords, Barnes And Nobel, iTunes, Android Google Play Store and on any other platforms, even on online libraries. At a certain point, you can create your own digital online library.

Creating an eBook is simple, you can write a book about a subject that you have a lot of knowledge of and you make your ideas come to life. Write a 50 page length book and publish it. You will be able to generate from 30$ to 200$ in average and in some cases, up to thousands of dollars each month.

The beauty is that, once you publish that book, you are finished, there is very little maintenance, you can update it any time you want, but that happens rarely. Most of the time you will leave it there and let it do the job for you. You can hire writers to write books for you, on any topic that you want, proofread the book, create or buy a book cover and upload it.

The more books you create, the greater your income will get from them. Let's say you publish 50 books in one year – which can be with 0 investments or if you buy the books and covers it could take you from 50$ a book, up to 1000$ if you write professional ones. For each book if you manage to obtain a minimum 20$ profit (which goes up to 200$ in average for a good quality and well written book), you will obtain at least 1000$/month. If you speed up the process, invest, hire writers and create an entire business in which you are the manager, things will get really interesting. There are people who make on Amazon thousands of dollars each month only by publishing books.

The main advantage here is that you can write it by your own, especially if you don't have any money and you want to start building your passive income business somehow. It's the perfect way to get started. The result is simple – you get a smaller or a bigger profit, no maintenance costs and no expenses, but this means that you have to know how to make an eBook cover or at least how to use an automated Cover Creator (like Amazon's Cover Creator Beta). You will also need to write in English without spelling errors, readers hate when they see grammatical errors, even though every writer makes some mistakes at some point. There is no such thing as perfection, keep that in mind.

You can also sell your book into multiple formats such as Paperback, Hardcover, Audible, CD or even DVD. All of these will help you maximize your sales.

With a few hours of daily work, enthusiasm and optimism, you will be able to generate 3000$/month after 1 year of activity on KDP (Kindle Direct Publishing).

The money you get from here can be reinvested in other passive income platforms.

Another method of generating passive income from selling informational products is from selling digital courses online – on Udemy, Skillshare or Clickbank.

All you need is a good niche (topic), a professional microphone, and a screen recording software for your PC – record a course as a software, convert it, edit it, advertise it and sell it on one of those platforms.

It's a harder task than writing an eBook, but it's a good way to spread out your income streams. Why not having 10 digital courses and 100 books at the same time?

There are people on Udemy who earn a fortune out of courses.

Now you will probably ask yourself what kind of courses sell on Udemy. Mostly any kind of niche, but the bestselling ones are tutorials – how to make money from web design, how to use Adobe Photoshop, how to edit video, how to use Microsoft Office, how to use Mac OS etc.

Be aware that education is getting more and more expensive, it's a lot cheaper to learn something by yourself directly from an eBook or from a digital course which you can access all the time, not one time like in an University.

EBooks will continue to dominate the market and outsell paperback books, as it's a lot cheaper, faster and environment friendly to sell digital books. No more trees will require to be cut, no taxes are added, to transport is required, delivery time is almost instant.

You can maximize profits even more by giving your products to affiliates, they will sell your products for a commission that you give to them (usually from 5 to 25%) and you can also advertise it by yourself. I will discuss more about affiliate marketing later on.

Chapter 6: Passive Income From Peer-To-Peer Lending

Few years ago, some wise people thought… what if… we build an online platform from which investors and people who need money fast could benefit. Based on this idea, huge platforms have been built, platforms such as http://zopa.com or http://lendingclub.com or http://prosper.com

These websites are certified, awarded by Forbes, CNN, New York Times and they got even other nominations and awards. It's 100% legal and profitable long term.

What is this all about?

You, the investor, invest money in this platform (you buy notes or credits) and you lend them to people who want to borrow money. In exchange, you will get a savings interest.

You can lend starting with (10-30 up to thousands, there is no limit). There are borrowers graded from A to G – A borrowers are safer to lend money, there is a high chance of these borrowers to make their monthly payments on time. G borrowers are more likely to miss some payments, they are classified as less serious borrowers.

Obviously, from A to G, there is a higher savings interest, from A borrowers you receive less than you would have received from G borrowers, but the risk is also higher. It is advisable to spread out your notes (25$ = 1 note or 1 credit) to multiple borrowers, you should avoid to give all your notes (all your money) to a single borrower.

On LendingClub, there is a demo on which for every 100,000$ invested into B borrowers for a 36 month period, you will get 3000$/month payment which you can withdraw or reinvest. It's up to you.

On Zopa, you can the highest savings interest is 5.1%/year for a 36 month period or more.

The point is that you can make a savings account through these platforms, instead of putting your money into a bank account, you can put a modest sum (10,000$ for example) into a lending platform and add 100-200$ / month for a 36 month period. You will have at the end of the 36 month period over 30,000$ which is nice.

You can calculate/configure your own money and how much you can earn from these platforms.

These online platforms have a lot of advantages for both borrowers and investors, money can be invested very quickly, money can be accessed by people who need a loan within a couple of days. You can get from 1000$ loan up to 300,000$ on some platforms.

It's a fast and secure way to invest your money in, the interest rates are higher than bank saving accounts and it's also much easier to operate everything online.

Chapter 7: Passive Income From Dividend Stocks

If you have money to invest in, you can go find a stock broker and start buying market shares from different companies such as Apple Inc., Hewlett Packard, Samsung, Amazon etc.

Let's take as an example Apple Inc.

For the last 3 months, if you would have invested into 300 market shares, you would have invested 300 x 109.41$ / market share and after no more than 3 months you would have earned 124.95$/market share which is a profit of 15.54$/market share and a total profit of 4662$ in 3 months which is in average 1554$/month.

So for an investment of 32,823$ (300 market shares) you get back 37,485$ in just 3 months if you want to sell them all. If we make an average, if you earn 1500$ month profit from those market shares that you have bought, you have a clear profit of 4.56% / month which is 54.72% profit per year. So, in average for every 100,000$ that you could invest in Apple stocks, you can earn 54,720$ clear profit.

Let's take another example from Apple. If you would have invested 5 years ago 1000 market shares, you would have paid 31.75$/market share, so a total of 31,750$ and you would have received back a total sum of 124.95$ which is a 93.2$ profit per market share and a total profit of 93,200$.

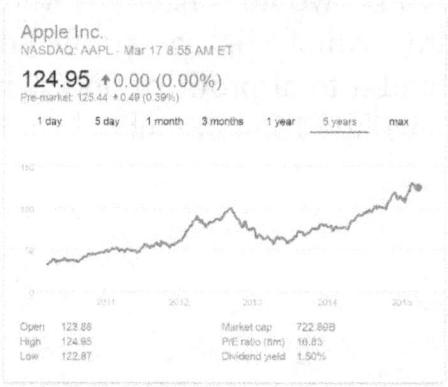

This transforms from 93,200$ / 5 years into 18,640$/year or again, as I said earlier, 1553$/month.

If you want to, you can sell only a part to take some profit and keep the rest of the stocks.

You can lose though, you have to be careful here, study the best companies and invest wisely.

Chapter 8: Passive Income From Websites And Affiliate Marketing

Have you ever seen a lot of annoying ads right all over a website, on most of the websites?

Behind those ads, there is an affiliate marketer who is just promoting his products or somebody else's products for a commission. A lot of other ads are put there automatically by Amazon, eBay, Yahoo or Google.

So how can you make money from creating websites?

You have 2 possibilities:

1. You create Niche websites – these are small websites (from 5 to 100 web pages) focused only on one specific Niche – you get a domain, you come up with a nice name related to the niche, you create your content and you put affiliate links – you have large variety of suppliers – Amazon, eBay, Google or any other platform. Most of the big companies have an affiliate program, after all, with the help of affiliates they can increase their profits.

For example, you can create Niche website which is based on extreme survival skills and accessories (have a look at Bear Grills). You can create articles, content referring to locations, places, objects, skills etc. and you will make a separate section with a small store (Amazon aStore) in which you put all the links to products available for sale. For instance, you can put hunting knives, tents, boots, waterproof jackets and other dozens of accessories and products. People who click on that link and buy something from Amazon (it doesn't have to be that product, if a person clicks on your link but buys something else through your link, you still get a commission).

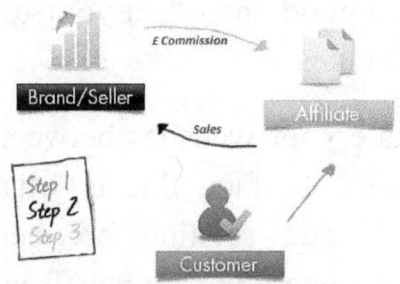

You can put automated Amazon links or even Google Ads, from which you are paid each month.

Then, you have to optimize your website using SEO, come up with ideas to bring a lot of traffic to your website. The more traffic you get, the more money you can make each month.

Once you have set your website, you are done, you can leave it there for a few months without doing anything and it will bring you money.

Who pays you? Google, Amazon etc. via paycheck or directly into your bank account. Sounds easy?

2. Authority Websites – these are bigger websites such as forums, blogs etc. and you can use them to add automated links, YouTube links, affiliate links of your own and so, even links to the Niche websites that you already own and from there send them to Amazon and you can make money.

Like niche websites, you will need to optimize the website using SEO, find a good name, get yourself a domain and whatever it takes.

It's like a chain, you relate your websites between them for your best results. In fact, this is what Passive Income is all about, relating between products, advertising and generating money from multiple streams, not just one.

Chapter 9: Passive Income From Savings Interest

The least profitable way to generate Passive Income would be to put your money into a bank account. You have to keep some money, you just can't invest all of it all the time.

Putting an amount of money into a bank account will bring you 3 – 5%/year savings interest, which isn't too much, but it is something. This means that for an amount of 100,000$ you will receive in one year 4,000$ (for example – 4% savings interest).

That is 333$/month profit – 100% passive income, you don't have to anything except going to the bank and put your money.

What I can say is that it isn't too profitable to keep a lot of money into a bank account, wise millionaires advise people to save to invest, not save to save. Even though it sounds well, you can't invest all your money, it has to be a balance between investing into something and saving into a bank account.

Numbers can vary, you can get less or you can get more, it depends on the bank's policy. But don't get tricked – usually, a bank with too high savings interest has less money or is in debt and so they encourage people to put money in that bank. Banks which are doing really well usually have lower savings interest.

Also don't forget, that the bank assures only a limited amount of money which is somewhere around 100,000$. So in case the banks goes into a fatal debt, the state guarantees you only 100,000$.

Chapter 10: Where to start from?

I suppose you have bought this book because you want to maximize your income, but you probably don't have too much money to invest into.

If money is your problem now, you should start with KDP – Kindle Direct Publishing. Outsource some books, write good quality books, upload them and results will start to come. Investments are zero or very low (a cover, an idea, a proofread).

If you want to proofread your book or create a budget cover for your book, go to http://fiverr.com and you will find there designers, proofreaders, even ghostwriters.

If you want to invest a little bit more and scale up your business, go to http://iWriter.com or http://odesk.com or http://elance.com or http://freelancer.com and find ghostwriters. Once you reach a decent income from these books, you can only be your own manager, give someone to write, someone to make a cover, someone to proofread, someone to give you an idea, put them all together and you are done.

You will probably ask yourself when are you going to see your first results.

To be honest, it takes 2 to 4 weeks to start seeing positive results with KDP.

Within a few months, you will be able to scale up this KDP business faster and at some point, you will generate hundreds even thousands of dollars each month.

As soon as you have reached a decent level number of books with KDP, you will probably want to expand, to make other things which can bring you money. Combine what you have learned by writing your books with digital courses. Create your own course, advertise it, sell it.

By uploading several digital courses on Udemy, you will be able to generate nearly 1000$/month from them.

Create a website to represent you, to advertise your books, courses and other products you may create in time.

Eventually, when you will generate a decent amount of passive income each month, you will be able to invest into lending programs, real estate properties to rent them or resell them after a couple of years and so, you will have a Passive Income Empire of your own. You travel, sleep, have fun and money will come into your bank account each month, without too much maintenance.

Let's sum up.

What you should start with:

1. Kindle Direct Publishing - Amazon
2. Digital Courses – Udemy
3. Create a website to promote yourself and even to do affiliate marketing.
4. Create niche websites of your own.
5. Expand all that you have built until now, enlarge your portofolio, make some your Amazon books available for printing or even as Audible books. Relate between all of your businesses. Promote your books trough your courses, your courses through your books, your products through your website.
6. Create an account on YouTube, Facebook, Twitter and any other Social Media Platforms to share what you do with as many people as possible. The bigger the audience, the higher your earnings will be. You can generate passive income using YouTube too – use affiliate links and monetize videos.
7. Save money to invest, invest in your freedom, don't waste money on things which have no benefits for you as a person.

8. When you manage to generate bigger amounts of money, buy real estate properties, rent them, resell them, reinvest.

Imagine what if...

- You have 100 published Kindle books and 20 books which are ready for printing.
- You own a website to promote different books, yourself, your courses, you have ads and links to other products.
- You have 10 niche websites which bring you from 300 to 500$ a month.
- You have 5 courses which bring you 800-1000$/month.

All of these are possible within one year, if you don't have any other activity (to do them full time).

With some work, optimism and patience, all of these can be achieved.

Conclusion

Managing to achieve financial freedom and even time freedom has recently become the ultimate challenge for people.

I hope I have opened your mind enough, get started using what I have explained, in that order.

"Nothing in the world can take the place of persistence. Talent will not; nothing is more common than unsuccessful men with talent. Genius will not; unrewarded genius is almost a proverb. Education will not; the world is full of educated derelicts. Persistence and determination alone are omnipotent. The slogan "Press On!" has solved and always will solve the problems of the human race." - *Calvin Coolidge*